# Bruce Wilkinson

# The 7 STAGES of SPIRITUAL GROWTH™

## PART ONE

*D*ear Friend,

Have you ever wished for a practical road map for your spiritual life? Have you ever looked for a tool that you could use for the rest of your life—so you could keep on track spiritually?

*The 7 Stages of Spiritual Growth* may be exactly what you have been looking for all these years! This course leads you through the predictable stages of spiritual growth from the moment you become a Christian until you reach an advanced, mature stage. Amazingly, over 90% of the participants said that when they learned the 7 Stages, they knew exactly where they were in their spiritual life and what they needed to do to grow to the next stage!

You are going to enjoy this course a great deal—and many of the questions you've heard about the spiritual life are going to become clear as we study God's Word together. When you are ready to move on even further, enjoy *The 7 Stages of Spiritual Growth* Part Two which will train you in the final four stages of your spiritual pilgrimage!

Bruce Wilkinson
Founder, Walk Thru the Bible

**PART ONE: Overview, Conversion, Consecration, and Conduct**

**PART TWO: Communion, Character, Core, and Convergence**

# CONTENTS

# HOW IT WORKS

This 12-session workbook (Part One) is composed of the first four units in the course: Overview, Conversion, Consecration, and Conduct. Each unit has three sessions focusing on the Principles of the Stage (Video), the Practice of the Stage (Video), and the Personalization of the Stage (Small Group).

**VIDEO**

## Session A
### Principles
**1**

#### Meaning, Misconceptions, Mindset

This video session lays the foundation for each stage and presents the meaning of the stage, the three common misconceptions about the stage, and the five main truths about the stage for your mindset.

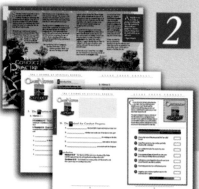

**2** ## Session B
### Practice
#### Milestones, Methods

**VIDEO**

This video session presents the five main milestones within each stage—from the initial milestone to the most mature, and then the overall method of how to grow deeper in the stage.

**NON VIDEO**

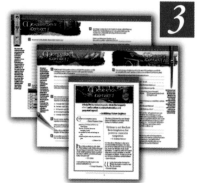

**3** ## Session C
### Personalization

This final session (non-video) is structured for maximum application. Through self-examination and group discussion you will take a measurement of your current progress in the stage, test your motivation to grow in the stage, and be challenged to take the next step forward in your mastery of the stage.

# OVERVIEW

have you ever been lost on a journey? With increasing frustration, you find yourself moving in circles. This is enough of an ordeal on a trip to a strange city, but what if it happens in life itself?

It needn't be that way. Life is about stages of transformation. The caterpillar struggles along, knowing that someday she'll fly away with lovely butterfly wings. You, too, are built for transformation, to move from stage to stage, becoming wiser and stronger. The Bible uses the language of milk and solid food—stages of feeding.

Those stages should be predictable. Spiritual growth has a rhyme and a reason. The first meaning of spiritual growth is this: we are to have a **relationship** with God. This is the reason we were created. There is no meaning without knowing Him.

The second meaning is that spiritual growth is your **transformation** into the image of Jesus. It happens inside *you*. You're intended to be transforming constantly, coming to resemble Christ more every day.

# OVERVIEW PRINCIPLES

The third meaning of spiritual growth is to enjoy the **expansion** of our dependent walk in God's Spirit. You can't simulate that or create it artificially. We are to walk in the Spirit, to be led by the Spirit, and to be guided by the Spirit.

Those are the meanings, but we must still guard against the misconceptions—for example, that our growth occurs through **methods we invent.** People seem to believe it's a do-it-yourself thing. But the path *to* God has been established *by* God.

The second misconception is that spiritual growth can come **without Christ,** the Word, or the Spirit. The Bible clearly tells us we come to God through Christ. We grow in Him through His Word, taught to us by His Spirit. The third misconception is that spiritual growth is **quick and painless**. It's most assuredly not! As we will discover, it takes great commitment and perseverance to travel down this path.

What, then, is the proper mindset for this journey? First, it **takes place by the Holy Spirit** within your life. Spiritual growth is the growth of your relationship with God, and it happens by the work of His Spirit. Secondly, spiritual growth can go **forward or backward**—or nowhere at all. Children experience growth spurts and plateaus. We do the same thing in the spiritual life.

Third, spiritual growth finds **constant opposition from satanic forces,** because the devil will do anything he can to prevent your spiritual growth. Fourth, spiritual growth best occurs when we're **involved in the local church.** Transformation comes as we use our gifts together, engage in Bible study and worship, and spur one another on. Fifth, spiritual growth is God's will for you, but it's **your responsibility**. God will not work in you without your consent and cooperation. You must work at it.

It may seem a bit intimidating, but it's worth the journey. God is calling out to you. You need only begin with the desire to know Him better—and an eagerness to experience this great adventure!

hunting God is a great adventure.
– Marie DeFloris

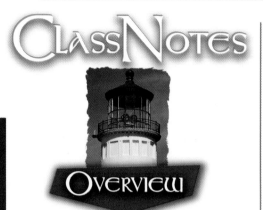

**Spiritual Growth erse**

2 CORINTHIANS 3:18 BUT WE ALL, WITH UNVEILED FACE, BEHOLDING AS IN A MIRROR THE GLORY OF THE LORD, ARE BEING TRANSFORMED INTO THE SAME IMAGE FROM GLORY TO GLORY, JUST AS BY THE SPIRIT OF THE LORD.

# Introduction

*Of whom we have much to say, and hard to explain, since you have become dull of hearing. For though by this time you ought to be teachers, you need someone to teach you again the first principles of the oracles of God; and you have come to need milk and not solid food.* Hebrews 5:11-12

# I. The Meaning of Spiritual Growth

## A. Spiritual Growth is the development of your relationship with _____

*Thus says the Lord: "Let not the wise man glory in his wisdom, let not the mighty man glory in his might, nor let the rich man glory in his riches; but let him who glories glory in this, that he understands and knows Me, that I am the Lord, exercising lovingkindness, judgment, and righteousness in the earth. For in these I delight," says the Lord.* Jeremiah 9:23-24

## B. Spiritual Growth is your transformation into the image of _____

*But we all, with unveiled face, beholding as in a mirror the glory of the Lord, are being transformed into the same image from glory to glory, just as by the Spirit of the Lord.* 2 Corinthians 3:18

## C. Spiritual Growth is the expansion of your dependent walk in the _____

*I say then: Walk in the Spirit...the fruit of the Spirit is love, joy, peace, longsuffering, kindness, goodness, faithfulness, gentleness, self-control...If we live in the Spirit, let us also walk in the Spirit.* Galatians 5:16, 22, 25

## II. The Misconceptions about Spiritual Growth

### A. Misconception #1:
**Spiritual Growth occurs through methods man** _____

*" 'And in vain they worship Me, teaching as doctrines the commandments of men.'*
*For laying aside the commandment of God, you hold the tradition of men…you reject the*
*commandment of God, that you may keep your tradition. Making the word of God of no*
*effect through your tradition which you have handed down. And many such things you do."*
Mark 7:7-9, 13

### B. Misconception #2:
**Spiritual Growth occurs without the Bible, Spirit, or** _____

*Jesus said to him, "I am the way, the truth, and the life. No one comes to the Father except*
*through Me." John 14:6*

*Jesus answered, "Most assuredly, I say to you, unless one is born of water and the Spirit, he*
*cannot enter the kingdom of God. That which is born of the flesh is flesh, and that which is*
*born of the Spirit is spirit. John 3:5-6*

*As newborn babes, desire the pure milk of the word, that you may grow thereby. 1 Peter 2:2*

### C. Misconception #3:
**Spiritual Growth is easy, quick, and** _____

*My brethren, count it all joy when you fall into various trials, knowing that the testing of your*
*faith produces patience. But let patience have its perfect work, that you may be perfect and*
*complete, lacking nothing. James 1:2-4*

## III. The Mindset of Spiritual Growth

### A. Spiritual Growth only takes place by the _____

*But the natural man does not receive the things of the Spirit of God, for they are foolishness to*
*him; nor can he know them, because they are spiritually discerned. 1 Corinthians 2:14*

### B. Spiritual Growth can be forward, backward, or _____

*But now after you have known God, or rather are known by God, how is it that you*
*turn again to the weak and beggarly elements, to which you desire again to be in*
*bondage? I am afraid for you, lest I have labored for you in vain. Galatians 4:9, 11*

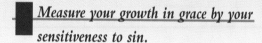

*Measure your growth in grace by your sensitiveness to sin.*

Oswald Chambers

**Session A**

### C. Spiritual Growth is consistently opposed by Satanic _____

*"The sower sows the word. And these are the ones by the wayside where the word is sown. And when they hear, Satan comes immediately and takes away the word that was sown in their hearts."* Mark 4:14–15

*Whose minds the god of this age has blinded....* 2 Corinthians 4:4

### D. Spiritual Growth occurs when we are involved in the Local _____

*And let us consider one another in order to stir up love and good works, not forsaking the assembling of ourselves together, as is the manner of some, but exhorting one another, and so much the more as you see the Day approaching.* Hebrews 10:24-25

### E. Spiritual Growth is the will of God but is your _____

*Be diligent to present yourself approved to God, a worker who does not need to be ashamed, rightly dividing the word of truth.* 2 Timothy 2:15

## Conclusion

*But without faith it is impossible to please Him, for he who comes to God must believe that He is, and that He is a rewarder of those who diligently seek Him.* Hebrews 11:6

**1.** If you were to interview ten different people on the street and ask them to describe the Spiritual Life, what three or four things would come up repeatedly in their answers?

_____

_____

_____

_____

**2.** Why do you think man is so inclined to invent his own methods to grow spiritually rather than using the ones outlined in the Bible? What would be two or three of the main methods that people around the world try to use today?

_____

_____

_____

**3.** Read Hebrews 5:11: "Of whom we have much to say, and hard to explain, since you have become dull of hearing." What are the reasons you think Christians can become "dull of hearing"? If a person came up to you after class today and said that they felt "dull of hearing" and wanted to change, what would you tell them to do?

_____

_____

_____

**4.** Read Hebrews 5:12: "For though by this time you ought to be teachers, you need someone to teach you again the first principles of the oracles of God; and you have come to need milk and not solid food." This verse reveals a surprising truth about spiritual growth, "by this time you ought to be teachers"—in other words, the Bible reveals a general timetable from spiritual birth to the point that every believer should teach another. Where would your best friends place you in this timetable of spiritual growth?

_____

_____

_____

**5.** Describe the time in your spiritual pilgrimage when you were growing the most in your spiritual life. How did you enjoy life during that period? What did you do that caused such growth? What would you have to do right now to regain and to surpass that earlier period in your spiritual growth?

_____

_____

_____

_____

L ife" is just another word for *process*. A baby moves through physical stages. A student moves through mental stages. A young married couple moves through emotional stages. And a Christian moves through spiritual stages, all of which which have seven key characteristics in common.

First, they're **predictable**, following a general path toward godliness. Second, the stages are for all **people**; they're not specific to any nation or age or gender or group, but for all of us. Third, the stages are **purposeful**. There is something essential in each one.

Fourth, the stages are **progressive**. Each one brings us to a higher level of godliness. Fifth, the stages are **perceivable**. We can know where we are in the process, and we can ascertain where others are as well. Thus, sixth, the stages are **profitable**. Knowing where we are makes it easier to get where we're going. And finally, these stages are very **personal**. We all walk the same path, but we walk it in the context of our lives and personalities.

What, then, are the stages? Here they are, in order:

**1. Conversion.** This occurs when a person turns to God, and puts his full trust in the death and resurrection of the Lord Jesus Christ for salvation—we must say "yes" to God and accept Christ's work instead of our own works. There are other names for conversion including being saved, being born again, being regenerated. But the idea is simple and inflexible—we must say "yes" to God and His provision for our salvation.

# OVERVIEW
# PRACTICE

**2. Consecration.** As believers who have experienced salvation, we soon realize that the Lord is requesting us to dedicate ourselves more fully to Him. The more dedicated we are to Him, the more consecrated.

**3. Conduct.** As saved, dedicated believers, we begin to see our behavior in a new light. Certain actions suddenly appear as they really are—*sin*. The Christian confesses his/her sins to God and learns to walk in greater holiness and obedience.

**4. Communion.** As we begin to behave in a new way, we discover that we yearn to know God better. We find new joy in deeper communion with God through prayer and His Word.

**5. Character.** Conduct, our outer behavior, draws us to know God inwardly—and that prompts Him to begin changing us inwardly. We begin to become more like Christ not just superficially but deeply.

**6. Core.** The change in our character seeps deeper into us—right to the very core of our being—right to our very essence, which is expressed in our true motives. Even in the Character stage, our motives might have been for self. But now we learn to live more frequently for the glory of God.

**7. Convergence.** Our life finally comes together. When our very motives have become godly, He can begin to use us as He has always intended. There's a deep feeling of "rightness" about life, of knowing why we were placed on earth. Everything fits—that's convergence.

> Wherever we are, it is but a stage on the way to somewhere else.
> – *Robert Louis Stevenson*

ClassNotes

Overview

**Spiritual Growth Verse**

2 CORINTHIANS 3:18 BUT WE ALL, WITH UNVEILED FACE, BEHOLDING AS IN A MIRROR THE GLORY OF THE LORD, ARE BEING TRANSFORMED INTO THE SAME IMAGE FROM GLORY TO GLORY, JUST AS BY THE SPIRIT OF THE LORD.

# Introduction

# I. The Characteristics of the 7 Stages

**A. The 7 Stages are** _____

**B. The 7 Stages are for all** _____

**C. The 7 Stages are** _____

*And we know that all things work together for good to those who love God, to those who are the called according to His purpose. For whom He foreknew, He also predestined to be conformed to the image of His Son....* Romans 8:28-29

**D. The 7 Stages are** _____

*For the earth yields crops by itself: first the blade, then the head, after that the full grain in the head.* Mark 4:28

**E. The 7 Stages are** _____

**F. The 7 Stages are** _____

**G. The 7 Stages are** _____

# II. The 7 Stages of Spiritual Growth

**A. Stage 1:** _____

*For God so loved the world that He gave His only begotten Son, that whoever believes in Him should not perish but have everlasting life. For God did not send His Son into the world to condemn the world, but that the world through Him might be saved. He who believes in Him is not condemned; but he who does not believe is condemned already, because he has not believed in the name of the only begotten Son of God. John 3:16-18*

**B. Stage 2:** _____

*I beseech you therefore, brethren, by the mercies of God, that you present your bodies a living sacrifice, holy, acceptable to God, which is your reasonable service. And do not be conformed to this world, but be transformed by the renewing of your mind, that you may prove what is that good and acceptable and perfect will of God. Romans 12:1-2*

**C. Stage 3:** _____

*But as He who called you is holy, you also be holy in all your conduct, because it is written, "Be holy, for I am holy." 1 Peter 1:15-16*

**D. Stage 4:** _____

*That which we have seen and heard we declare to you, that you also may have fellowship with us; and truly our fellowship is with the Father and with His Son Jesus Christ. 1 John 1:3*

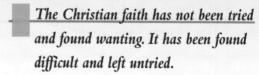

*The Christian faith has not been tried and found wanting. It has been found difficult and left untried.*

G. K. Chesterton

**Session B**

### E. Stage 5: _____

*And we know that all things work together for good to those who love God, to those who are the called according to His purpose. For whom He foreknew, He also predestined to be conformed to the image of His Son, that He might be the firstborn among many brethren.* Romans 8:28-29

### F. Stage 6: _____

*Therefore, whether you eat or drink, or whatever you do, do all to the glory of God.* 1 Corinthians 10:31

### G. Stage 7: _____

*Not that I have already attained, or am already perfected; but I press on, that I may lay hold of that for which Christ Jesus has also laid hold of me. Brethren, I do not count myself to have apprehended; but one thing I do, forgetting those things which are behind and reaching forward to those things which are ahead, I press toward the goal for the prize of the upward call of God in Christ Jesus.* Philippians 3:12-14

## Conclusion

**1.** Of all the 7 Stages of Spiritual Growth, which one do you think you are living in at this time? Why did you select that one?

_____

_____

_____

_____

ISCUSSION

OVERVIEW

**2.** Imagine 100 Christians from your local area all meeting on Saturday morning at a nearby hotel for breakfast. The speaker presents the 7 Stages and asks the people to select the stage they're in at the time. How many people do you think would be in each of the 7 Stages?

____ Stage 1: Conversion    ____ Stage 2: Consecration    ____ Stage 3: Conduct    ____ Stage 4: Communion

____ Stage 5: Character    ____ Stage 6: Core    ____ Stage 7: Convergence

**3.** Unless you have been exposed to *The 7 Stages of Spiritual Growth* before, much of what is taught may have been new to you. How do you feel at this point about the course? If you would have understood these stages when you were a new Christian, do you think it would have helped you, and if so, how?

_____

_____

**4.** This is going to be a bit more challenging of a question. Think through every person you know and select one person you think best characterizes each of the 7 Stages. For instance, who is the person you feel walks with God (Communion) the most? Write their names on the lines and share with the rest of the group why you selected them:

| Stage | Name | Primary Reason |
|---|---|---|
| Conversion | _____ | Why? _____ |
| Consecration | _____ | Why? _____ |
| Conduct | _____ | Why? _____ |
| Communion | _____ | Why? _____ |
| Character | _____ | Why? _____ |
| Core | _____ | Why? _____ |
| Convergence | _____ | Why? _____ |

**5.** It may surprise you, but perhaps someone you know selected you as the person who best characterizes one of those 7 Stages! Which stage would they have selected, and why do you think they would have selected you?

_____

_____

You've passed the first bend in the road in a life-changing journey—an exploration of the crucial stages of spiritual growth. It's a subject that invites some deep thinking, isn't it?

This is a course of study that cannot be approached with impersonal objectivity. As we started our discussion of the milestones of the spiritual journey, you surely found yourself making applications to your own life. That's because we're all deeply concerned about the issues of our souls— even when we're too busy or preoccupied to give it much thought. You're a spiritual creature by design, and when you're drawn to these topics it only means God's heart is breaking through, inviting you to the adventure of pursuing Him. He is beckoning you to the next stage in your spiritual growth.

So you've been learning about these concepts. You've measured yourself against the standards we've set out. What observations have you made? Are you excited? Discouraged? Eager to dig a little deeper? Perhaps the best course of action is to stop and measure your progress. That's what the Seven Stages Diagnostic on the next pages is all about.

We've designed this personal inventory to help you pinpoint your progress in the journey. This is one approach to quantifying where you are in your pilgrimage of spiritual growth.

For example, the first consideration is your basic position in the seven stages. It may be helpful to briefly review these:

**1. Conversion:** You're in the process of preparing to accept Christ as your Savior (or you've already accepted Christ).

**2. Consecration:** You're in the process of dedicating yourself to Him.

**3. Conduct:** You're in the process of conforming your behavior to His standards.

# OVERVIEW
# PERSONALIZATION

**4. Communion:** You're in the process of fellowshipping with Jesus Christ regularly and deeply.

**5. Character:** You're in the process of allowing the Lord to transform your inner self to become more and more like Christ.

**6. Core:** You're in the process of allowing Him to change your deepest motives.

**7. Convergence:** You're in the process of bringing all your time, talents and treasures to further the work of the Lord.

As you've followed the logical progression of the seven stages, you've probably experienced that flash of recognition that came when you said, "That's me! That's right where I am in my journey." Perhaps you're at Stage #2 and right on the border of #3. Perhaps you're stuck at #5 due to unresolved issues of #4. One purpose of this course is to help you know exactly where you are, where you're heading, and what you need to do to get there.

Our diagnostic examination will help you do that. Then you can take the next step in your spiritual journey. Before taking the inventory, be sure to take a few moments to pray. Ask God's Spirit to shine the spotlight on pertinent areas of your life—particularly the ones you're most reluctant to examine closely. Ask Him to help you answer honestly and thoughtfully.

You're about to learn a lot about yourself!

λ *humble knowledge of yourself is a surer way to God than a deep search after learning.*

*–Thomas à Kempis*

# MEASUREMENT
## OVERVIEW

This session does not have a video lesson but is meant for self examination and small group interaction and discussion.

**1.** In your own words, describe what the 7 Stages mean to you now:

_____

_____

_____

_____

_____

This session will enable you to locate your progress on the 7 Stages. Having studied and discussed two video programs on the 7 Stages, you are now prepared for an exciting session of self-discovery. Each question will help you apply the truths of the 7 Stages and then interact with other members of your group. Many of the truths will crystallize and you will find yourself experiencing a major spiritual breakthrough.

**2.** Break into your small group and from the last two sessions, fill in your Stage Description for each of the 7 Stages in the chart below. Discuss with your group each of the Stages until you have a good handle on each.

| The Seven Stages | | | |
|---|---|---|---|
| **Maturity** | **Stage #** | **Stage** | **Stage Description** |
| Advanced Stages | Stage #7 | Convergence | |
| | Stage #6 | Core | |
| | Stage #5 | Character | |
| Crisis Stage | Stage #4 | Communion | |
| Initial Stages | Stage #3 | Conduct | |
| | Stage #2 | Consecration | |
| | Stage #1 | Conversion | |

**3.** Write a short summary of which Stage best characterizes your Spiritual Pilgrimage at this point. Discuss your answer with the group and help each member identify their present Stage of Spiritual Growth.

_____

_____

_____

**4.** Write the Stage you are in at this time in the box on the left and the next Stage in the right box. Then break into pairs and interview the other person, trying to help them locate how far they have progressed toward the next Stage. When you both agree, each circle the box you feel best describes your progress to the next Stage (if you are halfway, then circle the 40-60% box).

| I am currently in Stage: | 0-20% | 20-40% | 40-60% | 60-80% | 80-100% | The next Stage is: |
|---|---|---|---|---|---|---|
|  |  |  |  |  |  |  |

**5.** Let's measure the pace at which you have been moving forward in the 7 Stages. Answer each of the following questions as best as you can— sometimes you won't know, so it will represent your best estimate:

a. Name your current Stage: _____

b. What is the present year: _____

c. What was the year you were born-again (if applicable): _____

d. How many years to grow to this Stage (b-c=d): _____

**6.** How then, would you best describe the pace at which you have been growing in your Spiritual Life since you started? Circle the appropriate answer:

a. No growth and even backwards at times
b. Slow with small spurts of growth here and there
c. Off and on—sometimes slow and sometimes steady
d. Steady with solid progress much of the time
e. Rapid growth and even major steps forward at times

**7.** In comparison with most of your friends and relatives, how would you best describe your growth in your spiritual life? Describe how your friends and family influence your spiritual life including positive or negative and discuss with the group:

_____

_____

_____

_____

_____

# MOTIVATION
## OVERVIEW

Now that you have measured your progress in the 7 Stages, the next step is to measure the degree of motivation you have toward growing to the next Stage. Look inside your heart and you'll discover the best predictor of your future growth: How much do you honestly desire to grow to the next Stage?

**1.** How would you best describe the level of motivation you've had in the past two to three years regarding making progress in your Spiritual Life?

_____

_____

_____

**2.** After learning about *The 7 Stages of Spiritual Growth* series, how do you feel about making progress at this point forward?

a. I strongly don't want to grow—I'm running backwards

b. I don't want to grow much, maybe here and there

c. I want to grow, but I'm not too sure if I'm ready to take any actions yet

d. I desire to grow quite a bit, and hope that I'll make some solid progress

e. I want to grow a lot, and am going to breakthrough!

**3.** Think through all your family, friends, and acquaintances and select the one person you believe has made the most progress toward complete Spiritual Maturity. What are the primary reasons you selected that person? And, what does their spiritual walk add to their life that you perhaps would like to add to yours?

Name of person: _____

Reason for selection: _____

What does Spiritual Maturity add to their life? _____

_____

Would you like to add that benefit to your life? _____

**4.** What would have to happen in your life for you to become highly motivated in becoming a person of deep Spiritual Maturity?

_____

_____

# Mastery
## Overview

**1.** How important is it for you to reach the 7th Stage of the Spiritual Life before you come to the end of your life? If you were at Stage 7 today, how would your life change?

_____

_____

**2.** Between each of the 7 Stages stands a major Spiritual Growth Hindrance. There are numerous different Hindrances but each of them must be overcome to experience true victory. Describe the Hindrance you must overcome to take the next step forward.

_____

_____

**3.** What steps would you have to take to overcome that Hindrance? In other words, how could you defeat it?

_____

_____

**4.** Victory in the Spiritual Life is available to anyone at any time, but there always is a price-tag. The Lord always wants His children to become more dedicated to Him, and He deeply desires that for you as well. Will you choose to take whatever steps are necessary to experience a major breakthrough in your life right now?

What would you have to do to breakthrough right now? _____

Will you commit to take that step of obedience? _____

By what date will you take that step? _____

**5.** Write out a short prayer to the Lord about your commitment. After all, your Spiritual Life is all about you and the Lord!

_____

_____

_____

# Meditation Overview

**Make sure the thing you're living for is worthy dying for.**
**— Charles Mayes**

Christianity is not devotion to work, or to a cause, or to a doctrine, but devotion to a person, the Lord Jesus Christ.
— OSWALD CHAMBERS

*There is simply no room for passivity in the Christian faith. Life in Christ is one long string of action verbs: grow…praise… love…learn…stretch…reach…put on…put off…press on…follow…hold…cleave… run…weep…produce…stand…fight.*
— JONI EARECKSON TADA

Christianity is the land of beginning again.
— W. A. CRISWELL

The pains of being a Christian are all growing pains, and growing pains beset only the growing!
— CHARLES SPURGEON

A Christian is never in a state of completion but always in the process of becoming.
— MARTIN LUTHER

I will not just live my life.
I will not just spend my life.
I will invest my life.
— HELEN KELLER

The great use of life is to spend it for something that outlasts it.
— WILLIAM JAMES

All growth that is not toward God is growing to decay.
— GEORGE MACDONALD

We grow spiritually through constant mortification of the natural man and constant renewal of the spiritual man.
— ADONIRAM J. GORDON

The deeper Christian life is the willingness to quit trying to use the Lord for our ends and to let Him work in us for His glory.
— A. W. TOZER

## To walk with God, we must run to God.
— GEORGE GRITTER

Christianity is either relevant all the time or useless anytime. It is not just a phase of life; it is life itself.
— RICHARD HALVERSON

The Christian life is not a way out, but a way through life.
— BILLY GRAHAM

STAGE 1

CONVERSION

You're walking toward your goal, and suddenly you stop—and turn. You move now toward a radically different (and very specific) destination.

Generally speaking, that's what the Bible means when it uses the word for conversion. Because of the sin that must be paid for by the death penalty, we are walking toward destruction. Like the Prodigal Son, we change direction, running home toward the Father. But it is the heart that turns homeward. That turn defines the starting line of our spiritual journey, and therefore it's important to eliminate several misconceptions about conversion.

The first misconception is that **conversion is unnecessary,** for various (false) reasons. For example, some say we will all be saved *(universalism)*, so why change? But the Bible teaches that Christ will come to separate the "sheep" from the "goats" and that not all people will enter into the kingdom of God. Others believe that life simply ends with death *(cessation).* But again, the Bible speaks of a "new heaven and a new earth," and of the dead rising to stand in judgment. Finally, others believe that a person lives and dies in an ongoing repetitive cycle *(reincarnation).* The Bible, however, tells us we live but once—and that conversion is the only hope we have.

A second misconception is that **we can create our own way of salvation.** People fabricate their own ideas of what it takes to be saved. The only problem, however, is that God, not man, determines the method by which one can enter heaven.

# CONVERSION
# PRINCIPLES

Clearing away these misconceptions, we seek the right mindset about conversion. The first is **a conversion problem**—that no matter how hard we try, we can't satisfy God with our actions. Works will never save us, because there is always sin, and because God's standard is perfection. Even the smallest sin qualifies us for the death penalty. And we can only solve that problem . . . by paying for that penalty.

The solution to that problem is the **conversion payment.** God the Father sent God the Son to deal with that problem. Because Jesus the Son lived without sin, He was eligible to take that death penalty we earned. He made the payment, and His resurrection was proof that the payment was sufficient. In taking our death penalty, He turned the tables and put death itself to death.

Third is the **conversion provision** which is the full and complete payment for our sin by the death of Jesus. The penalty for all of our sins—past, present and future—has been paid.

So how can we attain that salvation? We cannot. We need only receive it, for it is a gift. We can do nothing whatsoever to help pay for our salvation. It remains only for us to accept the gift with joy, live the abundant life, and begin to travel through the life-changing stages of spiritual growth. Jesus stood in our place; now we can begin to stand in His name.

> Conversion is not the repairing of the old building, but taking it all down and erecting a new structure. The sincere Christian is quite a new fabric, from the foundation to the topstone all new.
>
> —Joseph Alleine

**Session A**

### Conversion Verse

JOHN 3:16 "FOR GOD SO LOVED THE WORLD THAT HE GAVE HIS ONLY BEGOTTEN SON, THAT WHOEVER BELIEVES IN HIM SHOULD NOT PERISH BUT HAVE EVERLASTING LIFE."

# Introduction

## I. The Meaning of Conversion

**A. Conversion means to turn** _____towards_____

*And Jesus, immediately knowing in Himself that power had gone out of Him, turned around in the crowd and said, "Who touched My clothes?"* Mark 5:30

**B. Conversion is turning one's heart toward God for** _____Salvation_____

*So, being sent on their way by the church, they passed through Phoenicia and Samaria, describing the conversion of the Gentiles; and they caused great joy to all the brethren. "Therefore I judge that we should not trouble those from among the Gentiles who are turning to God."* Acts 15:3, 19

## II. The Misconceptions about Conversion

**A. Misconception #1: Conversion is unimportant and** _____

1. The Misconception of _____

   *All the nations will be gathered before Him, and He will separate them one from another, as a shepherd divides his sheep from the goats. And He will set the sheep on His right hand, but the goats on the left. Then the King will say to those on His right hand, "Come, you blessed of My Father, inherit the kingdom prepared for you from the foundation of the world." Then He will also say to those on the left hand, "Depart from Me, you cursed, into the everlasting fire prepared for the devil and his angels."* Matthew 25:32-34, 41

2. The Misconception of _____cessation_____

   *And I saw the dead, small and great, standing before God, and books were opened. And another book was opened, which is the Book of Life. And anyone not found written in the Book of Life was cast into the lake of fire.* Revelation 20:12a, 15

3. The Misconception of _____

*And as it is appointed for men to die once, but after this the judgment.* Hebrews 9:27

## B. Misconception #2: Conversion is possible through the method that I ___invent___

*Enter by the narrow gate; for wide is the gate and broad is the way that leads to destruction, and there are many who go in by it. Because narrow is the gate and difficult is the way which leads to life, and there are few who find it.* Matthew 7:13-14

*Jesus said to him, "I am the way, the truth, and the life. No one comes to the Father except through Me."* John 14:6

## C. Misconception #3: Conversion is impossible for many haven't heard about _____

*For the wrath of God is revealed from heaven against all ungodliness and unrighteousness of men, who suppress the truth in unrighteousness, because what may be known of God is manifest in them, for God has shown it to them. For since the creation of the world His invisible attributes are clearly seen, being understood by the things that are made, even His eternal power and Godhead, so that they are without excuse, because although they knew God, they did not glorify Him as God.* Romans 1:18-21a

# III. The Mindset for Conversion

## A. Conversion Problem: God established the penalty of sin to be ___Death___

*And the Lord God commanded the man, saying, "Of every tree of the garden you may freely eat; but of the tree of the knowledge of good and evil you shall not eat, for in the day that you eat of it you shall surely die."* Genesis 2:16-17

*For the wages of sin is death.* Romans 6:23a

## B. Conversion Payment: God sent Jesus to pay for our sins by His substitutionary ___Death on the cross___

*The next day John saw Jesus coming toward him, and said, "Behold! The Lamb of God who takes away the sin of the world!"* John 1:29

*Therefore My Father loves Me, because I lay down My life that I may take it again. No one takes it from Me, but I lay it down of Myself. I have power to lay it down, and I have power to take it again. This command I have received from My Father.* John 10:17-18

*But God demonstrates His own love toward us, in that while we were still sinners, Christ died for us.* Romans 5:8

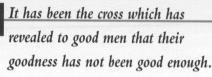

> *It has been the cross which has revealed to good men that their goodness has not been good enough.*
> – Johann Hieronymus Schroeder

### C. Conversion Provision: Jesus died for all the sins of all the world for all of _____

*And He Himself is the propitiation for our sins, and not for ours only but also for the whole world.* 1 John 2:2

*Surely He has borne our griefs and carried our sorrows; yet we esteemed Him stricken, smitten by God, and afflicted. But He was wounded for our transgressions, He was bruised for our iniquities; the chastisement for our peace was upon Him, and by His stripes we are healed. All we like sheep have gone astray; we have turned, every one, to his own way; and the Lord has laid on Him the iniquity of us all.* Isaiah 53:4-6

*And you, being dead in your trespasses and the uncircumcision of your flesh, He has made alive together with Him, having forgiven you all trespasses, having wiped out the handwriting of requirements that was against us, which was contrary to us. And He has taken it out of the way, having nailed it to the cross. Having disarmed principalities and powers, He made a public spectacle of them, triumphing over them in it.* Colossians 2:13-15

### D. Conversion Proof: God proved that Christ's Death was sufficient by the _____

*And if Christ is not risen, your faith is futile; you are still in your sins!* 1 Corinthians 15:17

*But this Man, after He had offered one sacrifice for sins forever, sat down at the right hand of God.* Hebrews 10:12

### E. Conversion Procedure: God invites everyone to believe on Jesus Christ to be ___saved___

*For by grace you have been saved through faith, and that not of yourselves; it is the gift of God, not of works, lest anyone should boast.* Ephesians 2:8-9

*And he brought them out and said, "Sirs, what must I do to be saved?" So they said, "Believe on the Lord Jesus Christ, and you will be saved...."* Acts 16:30-31

*"He who believes in the Son has everlasting life; and he who does not believe the Son shall not see life, but the wrath of God abides on him."* John 3:36

# Conclusion

*For God so loved the world that He gave His only begotten Son, that whoever believes in Him should not perish but have everlasting life.* John 3:16

**1.** Read John 3:3: "Jesus answered and said to him, 'Most assuredly, I say to you, unless one is born again, he cannot see the kingdom of God.'" Describe in your own words what you think Jesus meant by "born again." What exactly happens when one is born again?

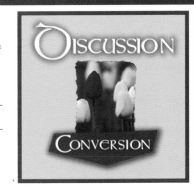

_____

_____

**2.** Jesus reveals one of the major reasons why people do not become "born-again" or "come to the light" in John 3:19-20: "And this is the condemnation, that the light has come into the world, and men loved darkness rather than light, because their deeds were evil. For everyone practicing evil hates the light and does not come to the light, lest his deeds should be exposed." Whenever a person is faced with the claims of Jesus, the Holy Spirit convicts them of sin (see John 16:8). At that moment, the person must choose either to come to the Lord and let his sin be exposed, or run from the Lord to hide and continue his sin. When you heard of the good news of Christ's death for you for the first time, did you come to the light or run into the darkness and hide? Discuss this in the group. Do you think that happens often?

_____

_____

**3.** It's utterly incredible that God reveals Himself to every single human being in such a way that everyone "understands" as outlined in Romans 1:19-21: "Because what may be known of God is manifest in them, for God has shown it to them...being understood by the things that are made, so that they are without excuse...although they knew God, they did not glorify Him as God...." If everyone "knows" God, why then does the Bible command us to tell others about God? For the Biblical answer, read Romans 10:9, 14: "That if you confess with your mouth the Lord Jesus and believe in your heart that God has raised Him from the dead, you will be saved. How then shall they call on Him in whom they have not believed? And how shall they believe in Him of whom they have not heard? And how shall they hear without a preacher?" The point of Conversion isn't to know about God, but to believe God raised Jesus Christ from the dead after He died for your sins. Describe your pilgrimage to Conversion. When did you move beyond believing in God to placing your full trust in the death of Jesus Christ for your salvation?

_____

_____

**4.** Many people struggle regarding whether or not their sins have been fully paid for by the death of Christ. When people come to know Christ as their Savior, they can believe He died for their past sins—but they often have a great deal of problem believing that He also died for their future sins. Why do you think that is true? Read Hebrews 10:12 to find the answer: "But this Man, after He had offered one sacrifice for sins forever, sat down at the right hand of God."

_____

_____

**5.** When do you think a person has "everlasting life"—when they believe or when they die? What are the implications of John 3:36 to a believer? "He who believes in the Son has everlasting life; and he who does not believe the Son shall not see life, but the wrath of God abides on him."

_____

_____

You're visiting the home of a millionaire and it happens: you tip over a priceless antique vase. It was worth more money than you could earn in 20 years, and your host is furious! Just then, a smiling stranger walks up and produces a box of jewelry. He removes several glittering diamonds—more than enough to pay for your damage. The millionaire's snarl softens into a delighted smile. His wrath melts away before your eyes. The Bible calls that propitiation. It happened when Christ paid the penalty for your sin.

All of us realize, deep in our hearts, that our terrible failures bring God's wrath. And we know it isn't in us to pay for the damage. But all at once, when Christ died on the cross in substitution for us, that wrath was fully melted. "It is finished," Jesus said—and He was profoundly accurate.

The ancient Hebrews dealt with their sin by offering a spotless lamb. The priest would move his hand over the lamb's head and symbolically place the sins on the animal's head; that placement was called imputation. Then the lamb had to be slain. Christ became the Lamb for us, with all our sins on His spotless head. Then God and His children could be "at one" again—atonement. It only now remains for those children to connect with God and make that atonement count. In doing so, we look for several milestones.

The first is to **admit** that we can't save ourselves. We realize that all our striving to

# CONVERSION PRACTICE

live well and do good is, at the end of the day, mere vanity. It can never fix the true problem deep down. We may scrub and scrub, but we'll never remove that spot of sin. We need to be rescued by someone who is spotless.

The second milestone, then, is to **agree** with God that Christ, His Son, is the one and only spotless Lamb who can take those sins upon His head. This milestone is known as repentance, and it means to change the mind. It's a breakthrough of the will.

The third step is to **accept** the gift that Christ has offered. We realize that we can do nothing, Christ has done everything, and we must simply say "yes" to the gift. It happens in a moment, and in that moment the miracle of conversion occurs.

Miracles are hard to believe. That's why we must **authenticate** what has occurred. We have to be certain. That's why the Bible reveals that God's Spirit will bear witness with our spirit that we are born again.

The final step in the Conversion Stage is to **apply** what we have experienced. We live the lives of new men and women, those who have turned around and begun to walk joyfully in a new direction. There are many adventures ahead, and each of them will change us more radically than the next. But none of them will come to pass without being preceded by this miracle of conversion.

> The cross is struck into the middle of the world, into the middle of time, into the middle of destiny. The cross is struck into the heart of God.
>
> —Frederick W. Norwood

**Conversion** **V**erse

JOHN 3:16 "FOR GOD SO LOVED THE
WORLD THAT HE GAVE HIS ONLY
BEGOTTEN SON, THAT WHOEVER
BELIEVES IN HIM SHOULD NOT PERISH
BUT HAVE EVERLASTING LIFE."

# **I**ntroduction

*Then He will also say to those on the left hand, "Depart from Me, you cursed, into the everlasting fire prepared for the devil and his angels."* Matthew 25:41

*Therefore, since we are the offspring of God, we ought not to think that the Divine Nature is like gold or silver or stone, something shaped by art and man's devising.* Acts 17:29

# I. The **N**eed for Conversion

## A. The Wrath of God is against all who _____

*Much more then, having now been justified by His blood, we shall be saved from wrath through Him. For if when we were enemies we were reconciled to God through the death of His Son, much more, having been reconciled, we shall be saved by His life.* Romans 5:9-10

*He who believes in the Son has everlasting life; and he who does not believe the Son shall not see life, but the wrath of God abides on him.* John 3:36

## B. The Wrath of God is satisfied by the death _____

**C. The Wrath of God when satisfied is described by** _____

*In this is love, not that we loved God, but that He loved us and sent His Son to be the propitiation for our sins.* 1 John 4:10

**D. The Wrath of God is fully satisfied because of the death of** _____

1. The Death of Christ paid for all _____

2. The Death of Christ occurred once for all _____

   *But this Man, after He had offered one sacrifice for sins forever, sat down at the right hand of God, from that time waiting till His enemies are made His footstool.* Hebrews 10:12-13

**E. The Death of Christ must be "connected" to each** _____

# II.  The Milestones in the Conversion Stage

**A. Milestone 1:**

_____ you are lost and can't save yourself

*For all have sinned and fall short of the glory of God.* Romans 3:23

**B. Milestone 2:**

_____ that you can only be saved through Christ's death

*For the wages of sin is death, but the gift of God is eternal life in Christ Jesus our Lord.* Romans 6:23

> To pass from estrangement from God to be a son of God is the basic fact of conversion. That altered relationship with God gives you an altered relationship with yourself, with your brother man, with nature, with the universe.
>
> Theodore of Tarsus

**Session B**

## C. Milestone 3:

_____ **Christ's death for your sins by faith**

*For by grace you have been saved through faith, and that not of yourselves; it is the gift of God, not of works, lest anyone should boast.* Ephesians 2:8-9

## D. Milestone 4:

_____ **that you were born again**

*The Spirit Himself bears witness with our spirit that we are children of God, and if children, then heirs—heirs of God and joint heirs with Christ, if indeed we suffer with Him, that we may also be glorified together.* Romans 8:16-17

## E. Milestone 5:

_____ **your salvation to grow spiritually**

*As newborn babes, desire the pure milk of the word, that you may grow thereby, if indeed you have tasted that the Lord is gracious.* 1 Peter 2:2-3

# Conclusion

*For God so loved the world that He gave His only begotten Son, that whoever believes in Him should not perish but have everlasting life.* John 3:16

**1.** Think back over the illustration of the man who hit the brand new car in the parking lot, and how the owner was propitiated by receiving all that money. At a certain point, the anger (or wrath) of the owner wasn't satisfied and at another point, that anger was fully appeased. How many "good works" must a non-Christian do in order to fully appease the wrath of God for his sins?

_____

_____

**2.** Who took the lead in solving the wrath of God? Did you? Did the angels? Or did God Himself? Since God took the lead and made provision for His own wrath, what would that reveal about God's desire to forgive the sinner? What price did God the Father have to pay to be able to forgive you? How does this make you feel towards God?

_____

_____

**3.** How much of God's wrath for our sins do you think was appeased by the death of Christ? For what percentage of all people from all time was God's wrath fully propitiated by Christ's death? Read the following verses carefully and underline the clues: (1 John 2:2) "And He Himself is the propitiation for our sins, and not for ours only but also for the whole world." (Hebrews 2:9) "But we see Jesus, who was made a little lower than the angels, for the suffering of death crowned with glory and honor, that He, by the grace of God, might taste death for everyone."

_____

_____

**4.** Since the Bible clearly states that Christ tasted death "for everyone" and was the propitiation for "the whole world," then doesn't this mean everyone's sins are already forgiven and they will automatically go to heaven? Think of it this way. God provided the complete remedy, all that needs to be done to "connect" the remedy to you is to "believe" that Christ's death is full payment for your sins. Do you believe that God wants you and everyone else in the world to believe? 2 Peter 3:9 reads: "The Lord is not slack concerning His promise, as some count slackness, but is longsuffering toward us, not willing that any should perish, but all should come to repentance." Therefore, is it the will of God that everyone put their faith in Jesus to receive the salvation accomplished by Jesus on the cross over 2,000 years ago? Since it is God's will, then why doesn't it happen? Share with the group the story about someone you know who refused to believe in Christ for salvation.

_____

_____

_____

**5.** Do you think a person who put their full trust in the death and resurrection of Jesus as full and complete payment for all of their sins can know that they are truly born-again and saved, or must always "hope" that they are? 1 John 5:13a reads: "These things I have written to you who believe in the name of the Son of God, that you may know that you have eternal life." Romans 8:16 reads: "The Spirit Himself bears witness with our spirit that we are children of God." How does the Spirit bear witness with your spirit that you are truly born again?

_____

_____

The time has come for another short test. Objective: to find out where you are on the issue of conversion.

This is an informal test, yet it echoes a more formal one—one which will stand as the greatest examination of your life. In the final analysis, each of us will stand before God to be tested on the very question that has been our focus during this unit: how do we deal with the problem of our personal sin? It's a "pass or fail" test, and the right score will bring you an eternity of joy; the wrong one will bring suffering beyond comprehension. That's why it's a good idea to give your full attention and concentration to the diagnostic exam on the following pages.

Let's review the discoveries we've made about conversion. We found that all people sense the hopeless plight of their sin, and the inevitable result of God's wrath. People respond in various ways. Many of them are deluded by false assumptions—that trying harder will bring salvation, or that death will be final, or conversely that death will simply give way to the next life and the next opportunity. But the Bible is firm in its teaching that we have this one life and we will be held accountable for it. It's also clear that our sin offends God and brings the death penalty.

That's why God engaged in a rescue mission. He sent His own Son, Jesus, to die for us and pay the penalty. He accepted our sentence of death so that we might receive His reward of life. Only because He lived without sin could He pay that price. But He did so, then defeated death itself.

# CONVERSION
# PERSONALIZATION

That's where you come in. Where do you stand today? Review the following milestones carefully. Think about the significance of each one. Then, determine whether your road has brought you to that particular milestone—and how you have responded. You'll want to spend some time in prayer first. Ask God to help you be honest with yourself. And finally, be willing to act on what you discover. (You may have already passed through all five milestones.)

**1. Admit**—that you can't save yourself. Have you come to this realization?

**2. Agree**—that Christ's death holds the only way to salvation. Have you made that acknowledgment?

**3. Accept**—the saving gift of Christ's death and resurrection. Have you said "yes" to God's gift?

**4. Authenticate**—that your salvation experience was genuine. Have you noticed significant changes in your heart toward God?

**5. Apply**—your conversion by living as a brand new creature, set free from the rule of sin. Has your life changed in a way that only conversion can explain?

Never in your life will it ever be more important to be honest with yourself. The third step, your acceptance of the gift of salvation, makes all the difference. It's the easiest test you'll ever take—you need only accept the gift that God provided—but it's also the most profound one.

> There are two kinds of people: those who say to God, "Thy will be done," and those to whom God says, "All right, have it your own way."
>
> – C. S. Lewis

# MEASUREMENT
## CONVERSION

This session does not have a video lesson but is meant for self examination and small group interaction and discussion.

**1.** In your own words, describe what Conversion means to you:

_____

_____

_____

_____

This session will enable you to locate your progress on the five Conversion Milestones. Having studied and discussed two programs on Conversion, you are now prepared for an exciting session of self-discovery. Each question will help you apply the truths of Conversion and then interact with other members of your group. Many of the truths will crystallize and you will find yourself experiencing a major spiritual breakthrough.

**2.** Break into your small group and, from the last two sessions, fill in your Milestone Description for each of the five Conversion Milestones in the chart below. Discuss with your group each of the Milestones until you have a good handle on each Milestone.

| Conversion Milestone Chart | | | |
|---|---|---|---|
| | STAGE # | MILESTONE | MILESTONE DESCRIPTION |
| Advanced Milestones | 1.5 | Apply | |
| | 1.4 | Authenticate | |
| Crisis Milestone | 1.3 | Accept | |
| Initial Milestones | 1.2 | Agree | |
| | 1.1 | Admit | |

**3.** Write a short summary of which Milestone best characterizes your Conversion at this point. Discuss your answer with the group and help each member identify their present Conversion Milestone.

_____

_____

_____

_____

**4.** Write the Conversion Milestone you are in at this time in the box on the left and the next Milestone in the box on the right. Then break into pairs and interview the other person, trying to help them locate how far they have progressed toward the next Milestone. When you both agree, circle the box you feel best describes your progress to the next Milestone (if you are halfway, then circle the 40-60% box).

| My Current Conversion Milestone: | 0-20% | 20-40% | 40-60% | 60-80% | 80-100% | The Next Conversion Milestone: |
|---|---|---|---|---|---|---|

**5.** Let's measure the pace at which you have been moving forward in the Conversion Stage (and maybe you are already finished). Answer each of the following questions as best as you can:

a. Name your current Conversion Milestone: _____

b. What is the present year: _____

c. What was the year you first heard the gospel: _____

d. How many years to grow to this Milestone (b-c=d): _____

**6.** How would you best describe the pace at which you have been growing toward your Conversion (if you have not yet been born again)? Circle the appropriate answer:

a. No growth and even backwards at times
b. Slow with small spurts of growth here and there
c. Off and on—sometimes slow and sometimes steady
d. Steady with solid progress much of the time
e. Rapid growth and even major steps forward at times

**7.** Think through your close friends and extended family, how many of them, would you say, are born again Christians or pursuing Conversion? Describe how your friends and family influence(d) your Conversion to the positive or negative and discuss with the group.

_____

_____

_____

# MOTIVATION

## CONVERSION

**Now that you have measured where you are in the Conversion Stage, if you have not been born again, the next step is to measure the degree of motivation you have toward growing toward your Conversion. Look inside your heart and you'll discover the best predictor of your future growth: How much do you honestly desire to grow in Conversion?**

**1.** How would you best describe the level of motivation you've had in the past two to three years regarding making progress toward your Conversion?

_____

_____

_____

_____

**2.** After learning about Conversion in *The 7 Stages of Spiritual Growth* series, how do you feel about making progress toward your Conversion at this point?

a. I strongly don't want to grow toward Conversion—I'm running backwards

b. I don't want to think about it much, maybe here and there

c. I want to consider it further, but I'm not ready to take any actions yet

d. I will give it careful consideration and hope that I'll make some solid progress

e. I want to experience Conversion at this time in my life!

**3.** Think through all your family, friends, and acquaintances and select the one person you believe has had the most dramatic conversion. What are the primary reasons you selected that person? And, what has been added to their life as a result of their conversion that you perhaps would like added to yours?

Name of person: _____

Reason for selection: _____

What has their Conversion added to their life? _____

_____

Would you like to add that benefit to your life? _____

**4.** If you haven't already trusted Jesus Christ as your Savior, what would have to happen for you to trust Him today?

_____

_____

_____

# MASTERY
## CONVERSION

**1.** How important is it for you to reach the 5th Conversion Milestone before you come to the end of your life? If you were at Milestone #5 today, how would your life change?

**2.** Between each of the Conversion Milestones stands a major Conversion Hindrance. There are numerous different Hindrances but each of them must be overcome to experience true victory. Describe the Conversion Hindrance you must overcome to take the next step forward.

**3.** What steps would you have to take to enjoy the freedom of overcoming that Conversion Hindrance? In other words, how could you defeat it?

**4.** Victory in Conversion is available to anyone at any time, but there always is a price-tag. Will you choose to make a personal commitment to take whatever steps are necessary to experience Conversion right now?

Are you convinced of your need to accept Christ for salvation?

Have you decided to put your trust in Him?

By what date will you take that step?

**5.** Write out a short prayer to the Lord about your Conversion.

# Meditation

## Conversion

**Conversion is so simple that the smallest child can be converted, but is so profound that the theologians throughout history have pondered the depth of its meaning.    – Billy Graham**

Salvation is free for you because Someone Else paid.

---

*A man can be regenerated, born again, only once, but he can be converted many times. Peter was a believer from the day he followed our Lord in Galilee, but he denied his Lord and for some days he was not a disciple although still a believer. Only after he was converted, turned from his perverse way back into the will of the Master, was he ready to strengthen the brethren and to feed the sheep.*

*— Vance Havner*

---

Blaise Pascal, one of the acknowledged masters of calculus, was asked why he believed in eternal salvation or eternal life. His remarks were as follows: "Let's assume that I am wrong and there is no life hereafter—then I have lost nothing. On the other hand, let's assume that I am right and there is life hereafter, then I have gained everything."

Conversion may occur in an instant, but the process of coming from sinfulness into a new life can be a long and arduous journey.

– CHUCK COLSON

A person may go to heaven without health, without riches, without honors, without learning, without friends; but he can never go there without Christ.

– JOHN DYER

### Jesus Christ burst from the grave and exploded in my heart.

– DONNA HOSFORD

If you believe what you like in the gospel, and reject what you don't like, it is not the gospel you believe, but yourself.

– SAINT AUGUSTINE

The knowledge of sin is the beginning of salvation.

– EPICURUS

STAGE

2

# CONSECRATION

**Session A**

Ten pennies are in your hand. Imagine they represent all the dedication in your life for God, for marriage, for career, and for entertainment and recreation. How would you divide those 10 pennies into each of those areas based upon your amount of dedication? An athlete who hopes to win an Olympic gold medal will dedicate himself or herself entirely to training and conditioning, and may ultimately stand among the greatest athletes in the world. They're sure about where to place the pennies!

Consecration is all about your dedication. You have some level of dedication to things you care about. As Christians, it's natural to give ourselves to Christ after we understand how He has given Himself to us. Unfortunately, too few Christians truly consecrate themselves. Often, people harbor one of three misconceptions.

First, they may have the false notion that **consecration occurs without a struggle**. They feel it should be relatively easy. But the Bible and mature Christians tell us that isn't the case at all.

Second, they may believe that **consecration is a one-time experience**. At some point of great emotion, they might have committed themselves to God, only to stall in their growth later. Consecration is an ongoing experience. We must continue dedicating ourselves to God—even daily.

Third, and perhaps most dangerous, is the misconception that **consecration is identical to conversion**. People feel that they dedicated themselves to God when they accepted Christ into their hearts. But these are two unique stages in the spiritual journey. Many people trust Jesus Christ the Lord for their salvation, but unfortunately, hold back from consecrating themselves until a later time.

# CONSECRATION
# PRINCIPLES

The Biblical mindset for consecration can be found in Romans 12:1, which reads, "I beseech you therefore, brethren, by the mercies of God, that you present your bodies a living sacrifice, holy, acceptable to God, which is your reasonable service." Five key ideas can be found here. The first is that **consecration is acceptable to God after you're born again**. It can only occur after conversion.

The second mindset is that **consecration is an official act of voluntary presentation**. We must, by an act of the will, take the initiative to present ourselves to God.

The third mindset is that **consecration is releasing to God complete control**. The idea is that we make ourselves living sacrifices—and that means that we die to ourselves and live to Him. In other words, we give God complete and unconditional control and obey His will.

The fourth mindset is that **genuine consecration is accepted and received by God**. We often believe that our sins make us unacceptable to Him. We think we must become near perfect before presenting ourselves to Him. But God finds us acceptable—just the way we are— because of the blood of Christ.

The final mindset is that **consecration is completely logical and reasonable to us**. It isn't a great leap in the darkness, but something we want to do. As believers, we know God and realize He is trustworthy. To reflect back over God's mercies to you brings that realization that consecration is the most reasonable thing we can do!

You are the one who distributes your quota of dedication. How do you want to spend your ten pennies?

*The difference between involvement and commitment is like a plate of ham and eggs. The chicken is involved—but the pig is totally committed.*

**Consecration Verse**

ROMANS 12:1 I BESEECH YOU, THEREFORE, BRETHREN, BY THE MERCIES OF GOD, THAT YOU PRESENT YOUR BODIES A LIVING SACRIFICE HOLY, ACCEPTABLE TO GOD WHICH IS YOUR REASONABLE SERVICE.

# Introduction

# I. The Meaning of Consecration

A. Consecration is the voluntary dedication of your life to _____

B. Consecration is a private commitment of the _____

# II. The Misconceptions about Consecration

A. Misconception #1:
Consecration occurs without _____

1. Missionary—sent to most horrible location (jungle or inner city)
2. Minister—have to preach and church every day—preach streets
3. Monk or Nun—live in some remote Monastery—helping sick
4. Martyr—great ridicule, rejection, suffering and even death
5. Moneyless and Poor—give up everything, live on street, bridge
6. Mindless and Robot—stop thinking and just believe
7. Miserable and Unhappy—life is boring, lacking challenge

## B. Misconception #2:
## Consecration is a one-time _____

   1. Consecration occurs at many different _____

   2. Consecration occurs at many different _____

   3. Consecration should occur _____

## C. Misconception #3:
## Consecration is the same as _____

   1. Consecration usually follows salvation by a number of years.

   2. Consecration is not required by God for salvation.

   3. Consecration radically influences one's conduct.

# III. The Mindset for Consecration

*I beseech you, therefore, brethren, by the mercies of God, that you present your bodies a living sacrifice, holy, acceptable to God which is your reasonable service. Romans 12:1*

## A. Consecration is acceptable to God after you are _____
*I beseech you, therefore, brethren*

## B. Consecration is an official act of voluntary _____
*That you present your bodies*

## C. Consecration is when you release to God complete _____
*A living sacrifice, holy*

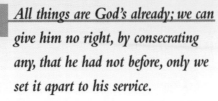

*All things are God's already; we can give him no right, by consecrating any, that he had not before, only we set it apart to his service.*

John Selden

**Session A**

D. Consecration that is genuine is received by God as _____

*Acceptable to God*

E. Consecration should be the completely logical and _____

*Which is your reasonable service; By the mercies of God*

# Conclusion

### A. Jesus was consecrated in His purpose

*"For I have come down from heaven, not to do My own will, but the will of Him who sent Me." John 6:38*

### B. Jesus was consecrated in His work

*"For the works which the Father has given Me to finish—the very works that I do—bear witness of Me, that the Father has sent Me." John 5:36b*

### C. Jesus was consecrated in His entire life

*"I lay down My life that I may take it again. No one takes it from Me, but I lay it down of Myself. I have power to lay it down, and I have power to take it again. This command I have received from My Father." John 10:17b-18*

**1.** Discuss with your small group the various things to which people are dedicated in today's society. List the top three. Why do you think people are so dedicated to each of those things?

#1 Dedication: _____

Why? _____

#2 Dedication: _____

Why? _____

#3 Dedication: _____

Why? _____

**2.** Twin boys of 19 stand outside your church. One is very dedicated to God and the other is very undedicated to God. If you had to take three guesses why the one boy chose to be undedicated, what would they be?

A. _____

B. _____

C. _____

**3.** How would your level of consecration influence your marriage, family, children and job?

_____

_____

**4.** Read Romans 12:1: "I beseech you therefore, brethren, by the mercies of God, that you present your bodies a living sacrifice, holy, acceptable to God, which is your reasonable service." Consecration should be something "reasonable" to you; in other words, it should make good sense or something is missing. This verse teaches that the "mercies of God" or the wonderful things He has and will do for you are the basis of Biblical consecration. List the top five things God has done for you as a person in your entire life:

1. _____

2. _____

3. _____

4. _____

5. _____

**5.** When was the last time that you took a significant step forward in your Consecration to God? What happened at that time? Do you sense your heart is warm to the thought of becoming more consecrated? What would have to happen for you to take the next step forward in Consecration this week?

_____

_____

_____

# CONSECRATION PRACTICE

If you were asked to reveal precisely where you stand on the issue of devotion to God, you might be very slow to answer. Many Christians aren't clear at all where they would be found on a gauge measuring consecration. But God could answer for each of us. He knows where we stand.

This is a journey that requires a good map, so we'll know exactly how many miles we've traveled and how many more remain. During this session we'll describe the milestones of consecration, and offer directions on how to find the right road.

The first milestone is when we basically live in **self-indulgence**. We have yet to realize what it means to live a life in devotion to Christ, so we remain devoted to ourselves— a self-defeating enterprise. The road must begin somewhere. The second milestone is just a bit farther along, and it comes when the Lord begins to send small tests—opportunities for us to be obedient to Him rather than our selfish desires. We're **strugglers** during this phase, striving to respond to God yet still bearing an allegiance to self. God will send tests that are very personal, difficult and unexpected. And they will offer the opportunity for a breakthrough to a deeper devotion to Him.

As we learn the painful lessons of obedience, we learn the meaning of **sacrifice**—the third milestone. We realize He doesn't want those things we're being asked to surrender; He wants us. We soften our grip on the things we've been holding onto, and we feel a great sense of relief. He requires us to put Him before all else.

The fourth milestone is **servanthood**. A person can be a servant of only one master. If the Lord is to be that master, we must present to him every person we know, declaring that God comes first. We must present to Him every possession we own, and every place He might send us. We must also present our position—any power and prestige we might attain. And finally, we must present to Him our purpose: the goals and dreams that can only be pursued if they are His will.

The final milestone on the road of consecration is becoming a **slave** to Christ. We take on this role voluntarily, out of utter devotion to the Master. In the New Testament, a bond slave gave up the right to become free; he had his ear pierced as a sign of being bound forever to the one he chose not to leave. Paul came to call himself this kind of slave. James did, too. And each of us can, at any time, present ourselves as free-will slaves forever to the only master who rules by unconditional love.

> *It costs much to obtain the power of the Spirit. It costs self-surrender and humiliation, and a yielding up of our most precious things to God. But when we are really in that power, we shall find this difference, that whereas before, it was hard for us to do the easiest things, now it is easy for us to do the hard things.*
>
> *– A. J. Gordon*

## Consecration Verse

ROMANS 12:1  I BESEECH YOU,
THEREFORE, BRETHREN, BY THE
MERCIES OF GOD, THAT YOU PRESENT
YOUR BODIES A LIVING SACRIFICE HOLY,
ACCEPTABLE TO GOD WHICH IS YOUR
REASONABLE SERVICE.

**Session B**

# Introduction

# I. The Milestones in the Consecration Stage

**A. Milestone 1:** _____

**B. Milestone 2:** _____

    1. Consecration Tests are _____

    2. Consecration Tests are _____

    3. Consecration Tests are _____

    4. Consecration Tests produce an inner _____

    5. Consecration Tests result in a consecration _____

## C. Milestone 3: _____

*I beseech you therefore, brethren, by the mercies of God, that you present your bodies a living sacrifice, holy, acceptable to God, which is your reasonable service.* Romans 12:1

## D. Milestone 4: _____

*Now great multitudes went with Him. And He turned and said to them, "If anyone comes to Me and does not hate his father and mother, wife and children, brothers and sisters, yes, and his own life also, he cannot be My disciple. And whoever does not bear his cross and come after Me cannot be My disciple. So likewise, whoever of you does not forsake all that he has cannot be My disciple."* Luke 14:25-27, 33

   1. Present to God every _____

   2. Present to God every _____

   3. Present to God every _____

   4. Present to God every position, prestige, and _____

   5. Present to God your life _____

## E. Milestone 5: _____

*If you buy a Hebrew servant, he shall serve six years; and in the seventh he shall go out free and pay nothing. But if the servant plainly says, "I love my master, my wife, and my children; I will not go out free," then his master shall bring him to the judges. He shall also bring him to the door, or to the doorpost, and his master shall pierce his ear with an awl; and he shall serve him forever.* Exodus 21:2, 5-6

   *1. Paul, a bondservant of Jesus Christ.* Romans 1:1a

   *2. Paul and Timothy, bondservants of Jesus Christ.* Philippians 1:1a

   *3. Paul, a bondservant of God and an apostle of Jesus Christ.* Titus 1:1a

   *4. James, a bondservant of God and of the Lord Jesus Christ.* James 1:1a

   *5. Simon Peter, a bondservant and apostle of Jesus Christ.* 2 Peter 1:1a

   *6. Jude, a bondservant of Jesus Christ.* Jude 1a

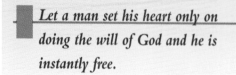

*Let a man set his heart only on doing the will of God and he is instantly free.*

A. W. Tozer

## II. The **M**ethod in the Consecration Stage

A. _____ what the Lord is asking you to consecrate

B. _____ carefully the costs

C. _____ to the Lord with someone or something to present

D _____ and transfer ownership and control as a sacrifice

E. _____ because the Lord receives your consecration as acceptable

## **C**onclusion

**1.** Estimate below the percentage of Christians that you know in your family and church and friends that would fit in each of the five milestones:

| Consecration Milestone | | Percentage |
|---|---|---|
| 2.5 | Slave | _____ |
| 2.4 | Servant | _____ |
| 2.3 | Sacrifice | _____ |
| 2.2 | Struggler | _____ |
| 2.1 | Self-Indulgent | _____ |

**2.** Why do you think Consecration is so strategic to the spiritual growth of all Christians? Discuss how the degree in which a person is consecrated would affect:

A. His or her conduct (*How one behaves?*)

_____

_____

B. His or her communion (*How one walks with God?*)

_____

_____

**3.** Think back over your life. Share with the group one of the Consecration Tests that you faced and how you did. What did you learn from this Test?

_____

_____

**4.** Which of the 5 Consecration Milestones did you feel best describes you in your pilgrimage right now? Share with the group why you selected that Milestone.

_____

_____

_____

**5.** Of the five areas that are to be consecrated to God (person, possession, place, power, and purpose), which one is the hardest for you? Why? Why do you feel it is "risky" or dangerous to dedicate this area to the Lord? At this time, what area of your life is the Lord encouraging you to consecrate to Him?

_____

_____

_____

_____

Consecration is perhaps the most strategic stage to the majority of Christians worldwide. The reason is simple: it is at this point in the journey that most Christians can become stuck in the quagmire, sometimes for years! Has that happened to you?

Consecration deepens when we realize He gave His all for us, and we spend a lifetime learning how to give our all back to Him. A great struggle often ensues, because we've conditioned ourselves to holding on, not giving in. But in time, if we persevere, we grow in our devotion. We move through other stages, but the holy business of consecration only concludes when we've given Him everything we have to give, including ourselves.

As you prepare to measure your own devotion to God, you'll want to review the important milestones in the consecration process. Begin to apply each of these to your life and faith.

1. Have you journeyed through the phase of **self-indulgence**? If this is where you find yourself, you're still almost totally devoted to your own interests. You seek to be the captain of your own ship, even when it comes to the things of God.

2. Have you journeyed through the phase of the **struggler**? You'll recognize it by the tests—small instances of God prodding you to give up something you cling to. He's less likely to send you across the world as a missionary, and more likely to ask you to offer some small possession you cherish.

3. Have you journeyed through the phase of **sacrifice**? This one is the turning point in all your striving to be more devoted to God,

# CONSECRATION
# PERSONALIZATION

for in this period you'll "get it" because you "give it." You'll suddenly understand that it's not your possessions God wants—it's you. Sacrifice will not be an occasion for resentment but for victory.

4. Have you journeyed through the phase of the **servant**? Now God is coming for the deeper things in your life—your people, your possessions, your places. You'll find yourself dedicating everyone you love, everything you own, and everywhere you go to God and His purposes. You'll present your position and your life purpose. You'll be tasting the deeper joy of devotion to God.

5. Have you reached the destination of the willing **slave**? If so, you'll discover one of the deeper paradoxes of the faith: you will have been so thoroughly set free that you'll sign away everything to bond yourself to Him. The ultimate freedom is slavery to Christ— you'll know the deep joy of that paradox.

Remember to pray before working through this portion of the Seven Stages Diagnostic. Ask God to show you exactly what issues have become obstacles to giving Him more of yourself. Reflect carefully on the inventory that follows. And trust God to apply these powerful truths to your life.

> If there is anything of power in the Salvation Army today, it is because God has all the adoration of my heart, all the power of my will, and all the influence of my life.
>
> —Gen. William Booth, founder, Salvation Army

# MEASUREMENT
## CONSECRATION

This session does not have a video lesson but is meant for self examination and small group interaction and discussion.

**1.** In your own words, describe what Consecration means to you:

This session will enable you to locate your progress on the five Consecration Milestones. Having studied and discussed two programs on Consecration, you are now prepared for an exciting session of self-discovery. Each question will help you apply the truths of Consecration and then interact with other members of your group. Many of the truths will crystallize and you will find yourself experiencing a major spiritual breakthrough.

**2.** Break into your small group and, from the last two sessions, fill in your Milestone Description for each of the five Consecration Milestones in the chart below. Discuss with your group each of the Milestones until you have a good handle on each Milestone.

| Consecration Milestone Chart | | | |
|---|---|---|---|
| | **STAGE #** | **MILESTONE** | **MILESTONE DESCRIPTION** |
| **Advanced Milestones** | 2.5 | Slave | |
| | 2.4 | Servant | |
| **Crisis Milestone** | 2.3 | Sacrifice | |
| **Initial Milestones** | 2.2 | Struggler | |
| | 2.1 | Self-Indulgent | |

**3.** Write a short summary of which Milestone best characterizes your Consecration at this point in your spiritual pilgrimage. Discuss your answer with the group and help each member identify their present Consecration Milestone.

60

**4.** Write the Consecration Milestone you are in at this time in the box on the left and the next Milestone in the box on the right. Then break into pairs and interview the other person, trying to help them locate how far they have progressed toward the next Milestone. When you both agree, circle the box you feel best describes your progress to the next Milestone (if you are halfway, then circle the 40-60% box).

| My Current Consecration Milestone: | 0-20% | 20-40% | 40-60% | 60-80% | 80-100% | The Next Consecration Milestone: |
|---|---|---|---|---|---|---|

**5.** Let's measure the pace at which you have been moving forward in the Consecration Stage. Answer each of the following questions as best as you can—sometimes you won't know, so it will represent your best estimate:

a. Name your current Consecration Milestone: _____

b. What is the present year: _____

c. What was the year you were born-again (if applicable): _____

d. How many years to grow to this Milestone (b-c=d): _____

**6.** How then, would you best describe the pace at which you have been growing in your Consecration since you started in your spiritual life? Circle the appropriate answer:
a. No growth and even backwards at times
b. Slow with small spurts of growth here and there
c. Off and on—sometimes slow and sometimes steady
d. Steady with solid progress much of the time
e. Rapid growth and even major steps forward at times

**7.** In comparison with most of your friends and relatives, how would you best describe your growth in Consecration? Describe how your friends and family influence your Consecration to the positive or negative and discuss with the group.

_____

_____

_____

_____

# MOTIVATION
## CONSECRATION

Now that you have measured your progress in Consecration, the next step is to measure the degree of motivation you have toward growing in your Consecration. Look inside your heart and you'll discover the best predictor of your future growth: How much do you honestly desire to grow in Consecration?

**1.** How would you best describe your level of motivation in the past two to three years regarding making progress in your Consecration?

_____

_____

_____

_____

**2.** After learning about Consecration in *The 7 Stages of Spiritual Growth* series, how do you feel about making progress in your Consecration at this point forward?
   a. I strongly don't want to grow in Consecration—I'm running backwards
   b. I don't want to grow much, maybe here and there
   c. I want to grow, but I'm not too sure if I'm ready to take any actions yet
   d. I desire to grow quite a bit, and hope that I'll make some solid progress
   e. I want to grow a lot in my Consecration and am going to breakthrough soon!

**3.** Think through all your family, friends, and acquaintances and select the one person you believe has made the most progress toward complete Consecration. What are the primary reasons you selected that person? And, what does their Consecration add to their life that you perhaps would like to add to yours?

Name of person:_____

Reason for selection: _____

What does Consecration add to their life? _____

_____

Would you like to add that benefit to your life?_____

**4.** What would have to happen in your life for you to become highly motivated in becoming a person of considerable Consecration?

_____

_____

# MASTERY
## CONSECRATION

**1.** How important is it for you to reach the 5th Consecration Milestone before you come to the end of your life? If you were at Milestone #5 today, how would your life change?

**2.** Between each of the Consecration Milestones stands a major Consecration Hindrance. There are numerous different Hindrances but each of them must be overcome to experience true victory. Describe the Consecration Hindrance you must overcome to take the next step forward.

**3.** What steps would you have to take to overcome that Consecration Hindrance? In other words, how could you defeat it?

**4.** Victory in Consecration is available to anyone at any time, but there always is a price-tag. The Lord always wants His children to become more dedicated to Him, and He deeply desires that for you as well. Will you choose to make a personal commitment to take whatever steps are necessary to experience a major Consecration breakthrough in your life right now?

What would you have to do to breakthrough right now? _____

Will you commit to take that step of obedience? _____

By what date will you take that step? _____

**5.** Write out a short prayer to the Lord about your commitment. After all, Consecration is truly between you and the Lord, and He needs to hear from you!

# Meditation
## Consecration

**Consecration is handing God a blank sheet to fill in with your name signed at the bottom.**
**– M. H. Miller**

The world has yet to see what God can do with and for and through and in a man who is fully and wholly consecrated to Christ.

> – Henry Varley

*Take my life and let it be,*

*consecrated, Lord to Thee;*

*Take my moments and my days—*

*Let them flow in ceaseless praise.*

> – Frances R. Havergal

Many of us are on the borders of consciousness—consciously serving, consciously devoted to God; all that is immature. The first stages of spiritual life are passed in conscientious carefulness; the mature life is lived in unconscious consecration.

> – Oswald Chambers

It does not take great men to do great things; it only takes consecrated men.
> – Phillips Brooks

Bring forth every thing separately—yourself, your family, your reputation, your property; relinquish all claim, and surrender the whole to God, to use and to enjoy them only as He directs, and with reference to His glory; never to withdraw what you solemnly covenant shall be only His.

> – R. S. Foster

Salvation is free, but discipleship costs everything we have.

> – Billy Graham

All to Jesus I surrender, all to Him
I freely give;
I will ever love and trust Him, in
His presence daily live.
I surrender all, I surrender all,
All to Thee, my blessed Savior,
I surrender all.

> – Winfield S. Weeden

STAGE

3

CONDUCT

Think of your life as a tree. It grows and branches out. It takes root in the right kind of soil. And we classify it by the fruit it produces. Another name for that fruit is conduct—the way we act and behave. If the tree of your life was shaken, what kind of fruit would fall? How much have you allowed Christ to transform your everyday behavior?

There are three common misconceptions about conduct. The first is that it's **automatically, instantly and completely changed** at conversion. Some believe that the moment they meet Christ, it's out with the old habits, in with the new. While the Holy Spirit creates a "new man" within us to live in

a new way, the "old man" simply won't die—he actually becomes more corrupt! Another misconception is that since we've been forgiven, our conduct **is free from God's present judgment**. But the Bible teaches that the consequences of our disobedience can be very grave indeed. A third misconception is that **it's easy to keep conduct in balance**. In truth, we struggle between legalism on one extreme and license on the other. It's often challenging to live in the freedom of Christ, but with wise restraint.

What is the mindset for holy conduct? First, it **results from salvation**. In Titus 2, Jesus tells us He died so that we might become eager to do good works. At the very heart of salvation lies the initiative for holy living. There are three key points in the process. One, we must put on the "new man,"

# CONDUCT PRINCIPLES

discarding the old, corrupt one like an old coat. We choose instead to wear the beautiful new one that is a gift of Christ. Secondly we must avoid, in the words of Romans 6, presenting our members to sin. These are parts of us that the devil would like to use for evil. Third, we must know that when we give into sin repeatedly, our conduct will dangerously slide into bondage.

That process of degeneration begins with the battlefield of temptation. It starts innocently enough, not with a sin but a **stumble**. We have the chance to brush away the temptation, but we should take note of the dangers of stumbling again. If we fail to do that, the temptation may return and lead to a **sin**. That's when we give in, consciously acting in disobedience. The next danger is

repetition. If we present our members to sin as a pattern of behavior, we find ourselves in a **snare**—a trap. Then we experience the difficulty of escaping the sin that has grown to be a **stronghold** that imprisons us. Finally, we can become a **slave** to that sin.

That's why it's good to know we have a choice! Our behavior is up to us. Galatians 5 tells us that the solution is to **walk in the Spirit**. When we live by that kind of power, sin loses its hold on us. The fruit of the tree is no longer sour but sweet. We begin to take on the conduct of Christ Himself, and we know we've grown through a crucial stage of spiritual growth.

> The serene, silent beauty of a holy life is the most powerful influence in the world, next to the might of the Spirit of God.
> – *Blaise Pascal*

**Conduct** **V**erse

1 PETER 1:15-17 AS HE WHO CALLED YOU IS HOLY, YOU ALSO BE HOLY IN ALL YOUR CONDUCT, BECAUSE IT IS WRITTEN, "BE HOLY, FOR I AM HOLY." AND IF YOU CALL ON THE FATHER, WHO WITHOUT PARTIALITY JUDGES ACCORDING TO EACH ONE'S WORK, CONDUCT YOURSELVES THROUGHOUT THE TIME OF YOUR STAY HERE IN FEAR.

# **I**ntroduction

*As obedient children, not conforming yourselves to the former lusts, as in your ignorance; but as He who called you is holy, you also be holy in all your conduct, because it is written, "Be holy, for I am holy." And if you call on the Father, who without partiality judges according to each one's work, conduct yourselves throughout the time of your stay here in fear.* 1 Peter 1:14-17

## I. The **M**eaning of Conduct

A. Conduct is the way one acts and _____

B. Conduct is either holy or unholy and fruitful or _____

*You also be holy in all your conduct.* 1 Peter 1:15b

## II. The **M**isconceptions about Conduct

A. Misconception #1:  Conduct is automatically, instantly, and completely changed at _____

*Therefore, if anyone is in Christ, he is a new creation; old things have passed away; behold, all things have become new.* 2 Corinthians 5:17

B. Misconception #2:  Conduct in the believer's life does not receive God's _____

*But let a man examine himself, and so let him eat of the bread and drink of the cup. For he who eats and drinks in an unworthy manner eats and drinks judgment to himself, not discerning the Lord's body. For this reason many are weak and sick among you, and many sleep. For if we would judge ourselves, we would not be judged. But when we are judged, we are chastened by the Lord, that we may not be condemned with the world.* 1 Corinthians 11:28-32

## C. Misconception #3:
**Conduct is easy to keep in** _____

1. The Pitfall of _____

2. The Pitfall of _____

# III. The **M**indset for Conduct

## A. Conduct that is holy and fruitful results from _____

*For the grace of God that brings salvation has appeared to all men, teaching us that, denying ungodliness and worldly lusts, we should live soberly, righteously, and godly in the present age, looking for the blessed hope and glorious appearing of our great God and Savior Jesus Christ, who gave Himself for us, that He might redeem us from every lawless deed and purify for Himself His own special people, zealous for good works.* Titus 2:11-14

*For by grace you have been saved through faith, and that not of yourselves; it is the gift of God, not of works, lest anyone should boast. For we are His workmanship, created in Christ Jesus for good works, which God prepared beforehand that we should walk in them.* Ephesians 2:8-10

## B. Conduct requires putting off the Old Man and putting on the New _____

*That you put off, concerning your former conduct, the old man which grows corrupt according to the deceitful lusts...and that you put on the new man which was created according to God, in true righteousness and holiness.* Ephesians 4:22-24

*Put off all these: anger, wrath, malice, blasphemy, filthy language out of your mouth. Put on tender mercies, kindness, humility, meekness, longsuffering; bearing with one another, and forgiving one another.* Colossians 3:8b, 12b-13a

## C. Conduct presents to God your members as Weapons of _____

*Therefore do not let sin reign in your mortal body, that you should obey it in its lusts. And do not present your members as instruments of unrighteousness to sin, but present yourselves to God...and your members as instruments of righteousness to God.* Romans 6:12-13

> **Jesus, like any good fisherman, first catches the fish; then He cleans them.**
>
> Mark Potter

### D. Conduct can degenerate through repeated sin into terrible _____

*Do you not know that to whom you present yourselves slaves to obey, you are that one's slave whom you obey, whether of sin leading to death, or of obedience leading to righteousness? For just as you presented your members as slaves of uncleanness, and of lawlessness leading to more lawlessness, so now present your members as slaves of righteousness for holiness.* Romans 6:16, 19b

1. Stage One: _____

2. Stage Two: _____

3. Stage Three: _____

4. Stage Four: _____

5. Stage Five: _____

### E. Conduct is controlled by the natural flesh or the supernatural _____

*I say then: Walk in the Spirit, and you shall not fulfill the lust of the flesh. For the flesh lusts against the Spirit, and the Spirit against the flesh; and these are contrary to one another, so that you do not do the things that you wish. Galatians 5:16–17*

*But the fruit of the Spirit is love, joy, peace, longsuffering, kindness, goodness, faithfulness, gentleness, self-control. Against such there is no law. Galatians 5:22-23*

## Conclusion

**1.** In which area of conduct do you think it is the hardest for men and then for women to live in godliness? Why did you select that conduct area for each?

A. Men _____

B. Women _____

**2.** Think about the Christians you know (including yourself) and put an "x" where you think their conduct would be located on the two conduct lines of holy/unholy and fruitful/unfruitful:

Unholy                                                                 Holy

| 0 | 10 | 20 | 30 | 40 | 50 | 60 | 70 | 80 | 90 | 100 |

Unfruitful                                                          Fruitful

| 0 | 10 | 20 | 30 | 40 | 50 | 60 | 70 | 80 | 90 | 100 |

**3.** Name three areas you have noticed in which the conduct of most born again Christians differs significantly from non-Christians and three in which it doesn't:

| Different Conduct than Non-Christians | Conduct the same as Non-Christians |
|---|---|
| 1. _____ | 1. _____ |
| 2. _____ | 2. _____ |
| 3. _____ | 3. _____ |

**4.** With which of the two extremes do you have more difficulty in your life—legalism (making up external rules that must be kept) or license (overemphasis on the love and grace of God and therefore living with carnal standards)? When you get trapped in that extreme, how does it affect you and those around you?

_____

_____

_____

**5.** Why do you think that a Christian does not sin when he has put on the New Man? If you were to practice this command in your life much more—to put off the Old Man and put on the New Man—how would your conduct change?

_____

_____

_____

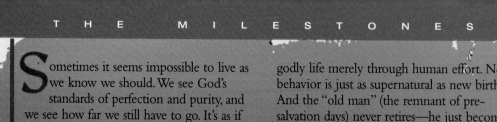

Session B

Sometimes it seems impossible to live as we know we should. We see God's standards of perfection and purity, and we see how far we still have to go. It's as if the goal is a rating of 100, and our names appear at about 14 on the graph. But God is patient. He wants us to remember that the holy life isn't built in a day.

We tend to get stuck because we try to carry the load on our own shoulders. That's a self-defeating strategy that can accomplish nothing other than frustration. The great mistake is to believe we can live the

godly life merely through human effort. New behavior is just as supernatural as new birth. And the "old man" (the remnant of pre-salvation days) never retires—he just becomes surlier than ever! It's important to takes things one step at a time, and here are the steps:

The first is for us to **purify** ourselves. As we accept Christ, we can later uncover unresolved sins and conflicts. From these we must cleanse ourselves. This involves repenting of those areas that do not please God, restoring damaged relationships, and resting in the Holy Spirit.

The second step is to allow the Lord to **prune** the branches of our lives so we can produce more good fruit. We let God clip away the things that would impede us from serving him.

# CONDUCT PRACTICE

Third, we **put off** the old life and **put on** the new one. In the previous session we compared these to an old, dirty coat and a beautiful new one. We will frequently catch ourselves putting on the old—and we must quickly change our thought patterns and actions.

The fourth step begins to see our lives become **productive**. We actively seek to please God. We desire to bear fruit in our lives, and we work at it. Finally, we reach the final step which is to walk in the Spirit—**peripateo** (the Greek word for "walk"). The word in Galatians 5 suggests the idea that we "keep on walking," as all the parts of our lives come together and mesh. We serve God with powerful impact.

So how do we get started? First, we **realize** that the "old man" can never bring the life we desire. Second, we **recognize** where we are and what we're doing that displeases God. Third, we **repent** when we stumble, turning away from sin. Fourth, we **relax** in the Spirit so that God can begin to live through us. Fifth, we **reprogram** our minds to see things more and more in the way that God sees them.

It helps to realize that Jesus has promised to reward us one day. We will each stand before Him and be recognized for our works. What basket of fruit will you present to the King that day?

> *A holy life is not an ascetic, or gloomy, or solitary life, but a life regulated by divine truth and faithfulness in Christian duty. It is living above the world while we are still in it.*
>
> *– Tryon Edwards*

Session B

**Conduct Verse**

1 Peter 1:15-17 But as He who called you is holy, you also be holy in all your conduct, because it is written, "Be holy, for I am holy." And if you call on the Father, who without partiality judges according to each one's work, conduct yourselves throughout the time of your stay here in fear.

# Introduction

*Let your light so shine before men, that they may see your good works and glorify your Father in heaven.* Matthew 5:16

*Beloved, I beg you as sojourners and pilgrims, abstain from fleshly lusts which war against the soul, having your conduct honorable among the Gentiles, that when they speak against you as evildoers, they may, by your good works which they observe, glorify God in the day of visitation.* 1 Peter 2:11-12

# I. The Milestones in the Conduct Stage

**A. Milestone 1:** _____

*Therefore, having these promises, beloved, let us cleanse ourselves from all filthiness of the flesh and spirit, perfecting holiness in the fear of God.* 2 Corinthians 7:1

*Therefore, if anyone cleanses himself from the latter, he will be a vessel for honor, sanctified and useful for the Master, prepared for every good work.* 2 Timothy 2:21

1. _____ the area that your conduct needs cleansing

2. _____ to the Lord about that area and confess previous sins

3. _____ any relationship that was damaged

4. _____ the Scriptures on that area on a daily basis

5. _____ actively on the Holy Spirit for holy conduct

## B. Milestone 2: _____

*Every branch that bears fruit He prunes, that it may bear more fruit.* John 15:2b

## C. Milestone 3: _____ — _____

*That you put off, concerning your former conduct, the old man which grows corrupt according to the deceitful lusts, and be renewed in the spirit of your mind, and that you put on the new man which was created according to God, in true righteousness and holiness.* Ephesians 4:22-24

*But now you yourselves are to put off all these: anger, wrath, malice, blasphemy, filthy language out of your mouth. Therefore, as the elect of God, holy and beloved, put on tender mercies, kindness, humility, meekness, longsuffering; bearing with one another, and forgiving one another, if anyone has a complaint against another; even as Christ forgave you, so you also must do.* Colossians 3:8, 12-13

## D. Milestone 4: _____

*You did not choose Me, but I chose you and appointed you that you should go and bear fruit, and that your fruit should remain, that whatever you ask the Father in My name He may give you.* John 15:16

*By this My Father is glorified, that you bear much fruit; so you will be My disciples.* John 15:8

## E. Milestone 5: _____

*I say then: Walk in the Spirit, and you shall not fulfill the lust of the flesh. For the flesh lusts against the Spirit, and the Spirit against the flesh; and these are contrary to one another, so that you do not do the things that you wish.* Galatians 5:16-17

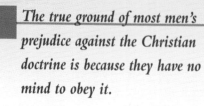

## II. The Method for Conduct Progress

A. _____ that your flesh cannot and will not obey God

B. _____ whether your works are of the flesh or the spirit

C. _____ for walking in the flesh

D. _____ and walk in the Spirit

E. _____ your mind with the Scriptures

## Conclusion

"For the Son of Man will come in the glory of His Father with His angels, and then He will reward each according to his works." Matthew 16:27

"And behold, I am coming quickly, and My reward is with Me, to give to every one according to his work." Revelation 22:12

**1.** Why do you think that when a person comes to know Christ as their personal Savior (Conversion) that God doesn't automatically make his conduct holy in all of his ways? At conversion, the Lord sometimes will supernaturally change one or more areas of a person's life. Did the Lord do that for you? If so, explain. If not, can you share with the group about another Christian who did experience such an "instantaneous" conduct change? (Read the story of Zacchaeus for a great example in Luke 19:1-10.)

_____

_____

**2.** Compare your conduct the year before you became born again with your conduct this year. What changes have you seen? If you aren't born again yet, then list the changes you would wish God would make in your conduct:

Change #1: _____

Change #2: _____

Change #3: _____

**3.** Read Matthew 6:33: "But seek first the kingdom of God and His righteousness, and all these things shall be added to you." Christ calls each of us to change our conduct so that it is focused on those things which are eternally important. This means that more of your time, treasure, and talents should be focused on this "first" as you grow in your conduct. Discuss the ways you have reprioritized your conduct to be more of a "first" Christian.

_____

_____

_____

**4.** Often conduct problems in a person's life are rooted in the extended family, not just the individual. Share with the group at least one major conduct problem in your extended family (don't reveal any damaging family secrets) that may be a snare or stronghold. How has that affected your life and family? How do you think that Conduct sin could be defeated?

_____

_____

_____

**5.** Discuss with the group how you have experienced victory in "walking in the Spirit" at various times in your life. Remember, the way you know you are "walking in the Spirit" is by the open and consistent display of "love, joy, peace, longsuffering, kindness, goodness, faithfulness, gentleness, and self-control." Share the specific things you did that worked for you.

_____

_____

_____

**Session C**

every stage of spiritual growth must be quantified in its own way. Conversion, for example, is best measured by a single word: the "yes" we utter to God. Consecration is measured by lifelong devotion. But Conduct may be the most measurable of all the stages. It's about outward actions, after all—observable behavior. People can watch you and evaluate your conduct.

The important things in life change the way we live. A daily job defines our schedule. Marriage and parenting guide our priorities. We make decisions and become new people based on our allegiances. If you're serious about your commitment to Christ, it will show in your behavior—not in radical, immediate change, but in a life that conforms itself a bit more each day to the image of Christ. Has your life been

changing? Are you more like Him than you were a year ago?

The time has come to test yourself in the area of conduct. As you prepare for the inventory that follows, carefully review each of the five stages of growth that a believer will always experience as he or she matures in Christian conduct. Locate yourself on the scale.

1. Have you **purified** your life? In this first stage, you begin the process of cleansing yourself from the accumulation of past, unconfessed sin. It didn't vanish magically at conversion; you must roll up your sleeves and do the "cleaning" to become the kind of vessel God's Spirit can use.

2. Have you **pruned** your life so that you focus more on that which is eternally important. Christ saved you so that you could do those things. And God must help you make more room to

# Conduct
# Personalization

bear fruit. By clipping away the distractions and misplaced priorities, God shapes your focus toward His priorities.

3. Have you **put off** the old values and the old conduct and **put on** the new ones? This is the conscious choice, made daily and in specific situations, to push back the "old man" and wear instead the robe of godliness.

4. Have you become more **productive** for God? If so, you are making a significant impact on the world around you. Your works are meaningful and you may have heard the applause of heaven!

5. Have you begun to practice **peripateo** (Greek word for "walk" in the Spirit)? This is a total integration of every area of conduct in your life under the power of the Holy Spirit. It all begins to work together as it was meant to be, and you "keep on walking." The "old man" is still a resident, but he's no longer a president! You live the righteous life with consistency, and you're a "difference-maker" for God in this world.

Where are you in the sequence? How close are you to the next step? Review each of these carefully, pray about them, and ask God to give you honest and reflective answers as you work through the diagnostic. Most of all, ask God to help you surrender the control of your conduct to Him. That's what spiritual growth is all about.

> N o one need live a minute longer as he is, because the Creator has endowed us with the ability to change.
> – J. C. Penney

# MEASUREMENT
## CONDUCT

This session does not have a video lesson but is meant for
self examination and small group interaction and discussion.

**1.** In your own words, describe what Conduct means to you:

_____

_____

_____

_____

This session will
enable you to locate
your progress on
the five Conduct
Milestones. Having
studied and
discussed two
programs on
Conduct, you are
now prepared for an
exciting session of
self-discovery. Each
question will help
you apply the truths
of Conduct and then
interact with other
members of your
group. Many of the
truths will
crystallize and you
will find yourself
experiencing a
major spiritual
breakthrough.

**2.** Break into your small group and, from the last two sessions, fill in your
Milestone Description for each of the five Conduct Milestones in the chart
below. Discuss with your group each of the Milestones until you have a good
handle on each Milestone.

| Conduct Milestone Chart | | | |
|---|---|---|---|
| | STAGE # | MILESTONE | MILESTONE DESCRIPTION |
| Advanced Milestones | 3.5 | Peripateo | |
| | 3.4 | Productive | |
| Crisis Milestone | 3.3 | Put Off-Put On | |
| Initial Milestones | 3.2 | Pruned | |
| | 3.1 | Purify | |

**3.** Write a short summary of which Milestone best characterizes your Conduct
at this point in your spiritual pilgrimage. Discuss your answer with the group
and help each member identify their present Conduct Milestone.

_____

_____

_____

_____

_____

**4.** Write the Conduct Milestone you are in at this time in the box on the left and the next Milestone in the box on the right. Then break into pairs and interview the other person, trying to help them locate how far they have progressed toward the next Milestone. When you both agree, circle the box you feel best describes your progress to the next Milestone (if you are halfway, then circle the 40-60% box).

| My Current Conduct Milestone: | 0-20% | 20-40% | 40-60% | 60-80% | 80-100% | The Next Conduct Milestone: |
|---|---|---|---|---|---|---|

**5.** Let's measure the pace at which you have been moving forward in the Conduct Stage. Answer each of the following questions as best as you can—sometimes you won't know, so it will represent your best estimate:

a. Name your current Conduct Milestone: _____

b. What is the present year: _____

c. What was the year you were born-again (if applicable): _____

d. How many years to grow to this Milestone (b-c=d): _____

**6.** How then, would you best describe the pace at which you have been growing in your Conduct since you started in your spiritual life? Circle the appropriate answer:

a. No growth and even backwards at times

b. Slow with small spurts of growth here and there

c. Off and on—sometimes slow and sometimes steady

d. Steady with solid progress much of the time

e. Rapid growth and even major steps forward at times

**7.** In comparison with most of your friends and relatives, how would you best describe your growth in Conduct? Describe how your friends and family influence your Conduct to the positive or negative and discuss with the group.

_____

_____

_____

_____

# MOTIVATION
## CONDUCT

Now that you have measured your progress in Conduct, the next step is to measure the degree of motivation you have toward growing in your Conduct. Look inside your heart and you'll discover the best predictor of your future growth: How much do you honestly desire to grow in Conduct?

**1.** How would you best describe your level of motivation in the past two to three years regarding making progress in your Conduct?

_____

_____

_____

_____

**2.** After learning about Conduct in *The 7 Stages of Spiritual Growth* series, how do you feel about making progress in your Conduct at this point forward?

   a. I strongly don't want to grow in Conduct—I'm running backwards

   b. I don't want to grow much, maybe here and there

   c. I want to grow, but I'm not too sure if I'm ready to take any actions yet

   d. I desire to grow quite a bit, and hope that I'll make some solid progress

   e. I want to grow a lot in my Conduct and am going to breakthrough soon!

**3.** Think through all your family, friends, and acquaintances and select the one person you believe has made the most progress toward complete Conduct. What are the primary reasons you selected that person? And, what does their Conduct add to their life that you perhaps would like to add to yours?

Name of person:_____

Reason for selection: _____

What does Conduct add to their life?_____

_____

Would you like to add that benefit to your life?_____

**4.** What would have to happen in your life for you to become highly motivated in becoming a person of considerable Conduct?

_____

_____

_____

# MASTERY CONDUCT

**1.** How important is it for you to reach the 5th Conduct Milestone before you come to the end of your life? If you were at Milestone #5 today, how would your life change?

_____

_____

**2.** Between each of the Conduct Milestones stands a major Conduct Hindrance. There are numerous different Hindrances but each of them must be overcome to experience true victory. Describe the Conduct Hindrance you must overcome to take the next step forward.

_____

_____

**3.** What steps would you have to take to overcome that Conduct Hindrance? In other words, how could you defeat it?

_____

_____

**4.** Victory in Conduct is available to anyone at any time, but there always is a price-tag. The Lord always wants His children to become more dedicated to Him, and He deeply desires that for you as well. Will you choose to make a personal commitment to take whatever steps are necessary to experience a major Conduct breakthrough in your life right now?

What would you have to do to breakthrough right now? _____

Will you commit to take that step of obedience? _____

By what date will you take that step? _____

**5.** Write out a short prayer to the Lord about your commitment. After all, Conduct is truly between you and the Lord, and He needs to hear from you!

_____

_____

# MEDITATION

## CONDUCT

**Holiness is not freedom from temptation, but power to overcome temptation.**

**– G. Campbell Morgan**

Conduct is an unspoken sermon.
— HENRI FREDERIC AMIEL

*Search me, O God, and know my heart today;*
*Try me, O Savior, know my thoughts, I pray.*
*See if there be some wicked way in me;*
*Cleanse me from every sin, and set me free.*

*– J. Edwin Orr*

how little people know who think that holiness is dull. When one meets the real thing, it is irresistible. If even 10% of the world's population had it, would not the whole world be converted and happy before the year's end?

– C. S. LEWIS

## Our Lord lived His life to give us the normal standard for ours.

– OSWALD CHAMBERS

It is time for us Christians to face up to our responsibility for holiness. Too often we say we are "defeated" by this or that sin. No, we are not defeated; we are simply disobedient. It might be well if we stopped using terms like victory and defeat to describe our progress in holiness. Rather we should use the terms obedience and disobedience.

– JERRY BRIDGES

## A holy life is a voice; it speaks when the tongue is silent and is either a constant attraction or a perpetual reproof.

– ARCHBISHOP ROBERT LEIGHTON

The kind of behavior that once brought shame and disgrace, now brings a book, movie, or a television contract.

– ANONYMOUS

When God purifies the heart by faith, the market is sacred as well as the sanctuary.

– MARTIN LUTHER